Who Did Grandpa Jobs Dream of Being?

Brave and Smart Heroes | Part One

GRANDPA JOBS

Daniel Gaba

Who Did Grandpa Jobs Dream of Being?
Brave and Smart Heroes | Part One

Self-Published by:
Daniel Gaba Studio

Copyright:
Text Copyright © 2024 Daniel Gaba Studio
Illustrations Copyright © 2024 Daniel Gaba Studio

ISBN: 978-965-597-018-0

Illustrated with love by: Olena Poronnik

Perfectly laid out by: Hila Segal

Written by your favorite book author: Daniel Gaba

Rights:
All rights reserved.
No part of this publication may be reproduced, stored in a retrieval system, or transmitted, in any form or by any means, electronic, mechanical, photocopying, recording, or otherwise, without the publisher's and copyright owner's prior permission.

Disclaimer:
All characters and events in this book are the product of the author's imagination.
Any similarity to real people, living or deceased, or actual events is purely coincidental and not intentional.
This work is intended solely for the entertainment and enlightenment of the reader and does not claim historical or documentary accuracy of any facts, places, or occupations described.

CONTENTS

MEET GRANDPA JOBS 4

LOCATION 1: Healthcare Hub 6
- Doctors 8
- Nurses 10
- Dentists 12
- Pharmacists 14
- Psychologists 16
- Vets 18
- Zookeepers 20

LOCATION 2: Security Base 22
- Police Officers 24
- Firefighters 26
- Soldiers 28
- Security Guards 30
- Lifeguards 32

LOCATION 3: Knowledge Center 34
- Teachers 36
- Historians 38
- Archeologists 40
- Journalists 42
- Translators 44
- Writers 46
- Scientists 48

A MESSAGE FROM GRANDPA JOBS 50

ANIMAL CONNECTIONS FOR THE MOST CURIOUS 52

Hello, my friend! My name is **Grandpa Jobs**. Nice to meet you!

My story began with a passion for dreaming and making new friends. Throughout my life, I traveled to amazing parts of our planet and even beyond its borders and met many new friends— each one a real master of their craft.

Ever since I was a kid, I have been interested in many different professions (that's a big word that means jobs), and my new friends allowed me to try theirs for a while.

As a result of my travels, I have gathered a large collection of jobs that I want to share with you so you can think about your future and find your favorite job too.

Tell me your name, and let's start our exciting journey through the world of professions! In this book, we will visit the **Healthcare Hub**, the **Security Base**, and the **Knowledge Center**.

Let's get started!

P.S. Actually, before we start our amazing adventure, I want to tell you that in the drawings included in these pages, I have hidden some interesting facts about the most outstanding people in these jobs, such as appearances, inventions, favorite hobbies, or incredible prizes they won.

Your challenge in this book is to find these little details and get to know these people better.

P.P.S. One more thing, my young friend: in this book, you will find that each job is linked to an animal. This is no accident.

Try to guess the connection between the professions and the animals, and if your curiosity takes over, you will find the answers on page 52.

LET'S GO ON AN ADVENTURE!

Hello, Dr. Hopkins! What adventures await us in the Healthcare Hub today?

Hi, Grandpa Jobs! Today, we will meet the heroes of healthcare—doctors, nurses, and many more who help keep us all healthy.

Just think—maybe one day our young reader will become one of these heroes, helping people feel better!

Let's turn the page, and together, we'll explore the world of healthcare.

Hello, little doc! We are Alexander and Virginia, and we are DOCTORS

Our Key Responsibilities:
As doctors, we spend our days diagnosing illnesses and prescribing treatments to help people feel better. We also perform check-ups to monitor the health of our patients and prevent future illnesses.

Why We Love Our Job:
Helping people recover from sickness and maintaining their health brings us immense satisfaction. Seeing the relief and happiness on someone's face when they get better is truly rewarding.

Find Your Path:
Some doctors take care of kids, others look after our hearts, and some even perform surgeries, each focusing on different types of care and treatment. We can work in hospitals and clinics or research new cures.

How to Become One of Us?
To become a doctor, you must complete many years of medical school followed by hands-on training. It requires a strong foundation in science and a deep commitment to caring for others.

A Question for You:
Would you like to wear a white coat and use a stethoscope to help people stay healthy one day, as a doctor?

Alexander researches, Virginia cares,
In their mission, nothing compares.
With knowledge vast and hearts so true,
They heal the old and tend the new.

Hey, little caretaker! You can call us Florence and Luther, and we are
NURSES

Our Key Responsibilities:
As nurses, we take care of people when they're sick, making sure they feel better. We also assist doctors in their work, providing support and care to ensure the best treatment for every patient.

Why We Love Our Job:
Helping people smile and get better is the best part of our day. It feels amazing to see someone go home happy and healthy because of our help.

Find Your Path:
Nursing is not just about working in a hospital; nurses can work in schools or community centers, and even travel around the world to help others. We can specialize in taking care of babies, helping people with heart problems, or even teaching others about health.

How to Become One of Us?
To become a nurse, you need to study nursing in school and learn all about the human body and how to take care of it. It's important to be kind, patient, and good at listening to others.

A Question for You:
Would you like to become a nurse and help people feel healthy and happy one day?

Side by side, they face each day,
With smiles that chase the clouds away.
Luther and Florence, with hands so kind,
Heal the body, ease the mind.

Hi there, bright smile! We are Greene and Minnie, and we are
DENTISTS

Our Key Responsibilities:
We look after people's teeth, making sure they have bright smiles and healthy gums. We also teach kids and adults how to brush and floss properly to keep their teeth strong.

Why We Love Our Job:
It's great seeing someone smile with confidence after we've helped take care of their teeth. Plus, teaching others how to maintain their dental health is rewarding.

Find Your Path:
Dentistry isn't just about checking teeth; there are many specialties, like orthodontics for straightening teeth, pediatric dentistry for kids, and even cosmetic dentistry for those looking for a dazzling smile.

How to Become One of Us?
To become a dentist, you need to study dentistry in college, learning all about teeth and how to care for them. It's important to have a steady hand and enjoy helping others feel good about their smiles.

A Question for You:
Would you like to explore the world of smiles and become a hero in dental care as a dentist one day?

Greene and Minnie, in their clinic bright,
Turn dental visits into delight.
With precision, care, and skillful touch,
They ensure their patients don't fear much.

Hi, little healer! We are Friedrich and Gertrude, and we work as
PHARMACISTS

Our Key Responsibilities:
As pharmacists, we make sure people get the right medicines to help them feel better. We also teach them how to use their medicine safely and effectively.

Why We Love Our Job:
Helping people understand their health better and seeing them recover brings us a lot of happiness. Plus, it's exciting to learn about all the new medicines and how they can improve lives.

Find Your Path:
Pharmacists work in many places, not just pharmacies. Some of us work in hospitals, research labs, or companies making new medicines, so there's always something new to explore.

How to Become One of Us?
Becoming a pharmacist starts with a strong foundation in subjects like biology and chemistry in school. Then, you'll need to study pharmacy at a university, where you'll gain the knowledge and skills to guide others in taking care of their health.

A Question for You:
Would you like to be the one who knows all about medicines and helps people feel their best one day?

Friedrich and Gertrude, with knowledge vast,
Fill prescriptions, quick and fast.
In the realm of pills and potions they reign,
Easing discomfort, reducing pain.

Hello, young thinker! I'm Sigmund and this is my friend Melanie, and we are PSYCHOLOGISTS

Our Key Responsibilities:
As psychologists, we listen to people's thoughts and feelings to help them understand themselves better.
We use special techniques to support them in overcoming challenges and improving their mental health.

Why We Love Our Job:
We love being a psychologist because we can make a real difference in someone's life by offering guidance and support. It's incredibly rewarding to see someone grow and find happiness through our meetings together.

Find Your Path:
Psychology is a vast field with many specialties, from working with children in schools to helping adults in private practice. Some psychologists conduct research or teach at universities, so there are many paths to explore.

How to Become One of Us?
To be a psychologist, you'll need to be genuinely interested in human behavior and emotions. You'll need to earn a psychology degree in college and then further your studies with advanced degrees, depending on the area of psychology you're passionate about.

A Question for You:
Do you dream of unlocking the mysteries of the mind and being someone's hero by guiding them to happiness as a psychologist?

Sigmund and Melanie, with minds so keen,
Explore the depths of the unseen.
In their rooms, where secrets unfold,
They listen to stories, new and old.

Hello, little animal lover! I'm Sophia and this is my colleague Claude, and we are **VETS**

Our Key Responsibilities:
As veterinarians, we care for animals of all sizes, from tiny hamsters to large horses. We diagnose their illnesses, treat injuries, and perform surgeries to keep them healthy and happy.

Why We Love Our Job:
We adore being vets because every day we get to help animals feel better and ensure they lead long, joyful lives. Seeing the relief and happiness in both the animals and their owners' eyes is the best reward.

Find Your Path:
The veterinary field is broad, with roles in clinics caring for pets, working at zoos with exotic animals, or even researching new treatments for animal diseases. There's a special niche for everyone who loves animals.

How to Become One of Us?
If you're interested in becoming a veterinarian, start by loving and learning about different kinds of animals. You'll need to study biology and other sciences in school, then attend veterinary school to gain the skills to care for animal health.

A Question for You:
Imagine being a superhero for animals, healing them, and making tails wag with joy. Would you like to be a veterinarian and join this adventure?

Claude and Sophia, with hearts so wide,
Care for the creatures by their side.
They heal with skill, both fur and feather,
On sunny days and in stormy weather.

Giant Panda

Hello, little one! Our names are Steve and Jane, and we are ZOOKEEPERS

Our Key Responsibilities:
Our job is to take care of the animals at the zoo, making sure they have everything they need to be happy and healthy. We feed them, clean their homes, and sometimes even play with them to keep them active and engaged.

Why We Love Our Job:
We love being zookeepers because every day we get to be close to some of the most amazing animals from all over the world. It's incredibly fulfilling to form bonds with these creatures and contribute to their well-being and conservation.

Find Your Path:
Being a zookeeper isn't just about looking after animals; it's also about educating visitors on wildlife conservation and conducting research to help protect endangered species.

How to Become One of Us?
If you dream of becoming a zookeeper, get curious about nature and all kinds of animals. Studying biology or zoology in school can help you, and getting experience through volunteering at zoos or animal shelters is a great way to start your journey.

A Question for You:
Would you like to care for lions, monkeys, and elephants as a zookeeper, becoming their friend and protector?

Together, they feed, clean, and play,
Making sure the animals are okay.
Steve and Jane, with gentle hands,
Fulfill each animal's unique demands.

Hello there, Grandpa Jobs! Today, we will discover the brave world of security—where dedicated professionals work daily to keep us safe.

What if someday the young reader gets to become a hero just like them, helping everyone stay safe?

Let's turn the page, and together, we'll explore the world of bravery.

★ Snapping Shrimp ★

Hey, young hero! We are Alice and Robert, and we are
POLICE OFFICERS

Our Key Responsibilities:
As police officers, we help keep our streets safe by making sure everyone follows the rules. We also help people who are in trouble and need assistance.

Why We Love Our Job:
We love being police officers because we get to protect and serve our community. It makes us happy to see people safe and to help them feel secure.

Find Your Path:
In the police force, there are many different roles. Some officers work with dogs to find things, while others help solve mysteries as detectives.

How to Become One of Us?
To become a police officer, you need to study hard in school and learn a lot about the law. After that, you'll go to a special police academy where you can receive training to keep people safe. Being strong and healthy is also very important.

A Question for You:
Would you like to drive a police car with flashing lights and help keep your city safe one day as a police officer?

Alice and Robert, in uniform blue,
Stand for justice, strong and true.
In the community, they build trust,
Their approach, fair and just.

Hi there, brave spark! I am Raymond—and I am Brenda—and we are

FIREFIGHTERS

Our Key Responsibilities:
We rush to the rescue whenever there's a fire, working with our team to put it out and save lives. We also teach people how to be safe and prevent fires from happening.

Why We Love Our Job:
Being a firefighter is amazing because we get to be a real-life hero. We help people every day, and there's nothing better than knowing we've made a difference.

Find Your Path:
Firefighting isn't just about fighting fires; we also respond to other emergencies, like car accidents or natural disasters. Some of us even specialize in rescuing animals or teaching fire safety.

How to Become One of Us?
To become a firefighter, you need strength, courage, and a willingness to learn. Alongside tackling fires, you'll be trained as a first responder, including how to perform life-saving CPR. This will prepare you to handle all kinds of emergencies.

A Question for You:
Do you dream of sliding down the fire pole and rushing off in a firetruck to save the day as a firefighter?

Raymond and Brenda, with hoses in hand,
Stand as protectors of the land.
In helmets and gear, they charge ahead,
To save lives where many wouldn't dare tread.

Black Rhinoceros

Greetings, little warrior!
I'm Audie, and this is my comrade Lyudmila, and we are
SOLDIERS

Our Key Responsibilities:
As soldiers, we protect our country and its people by being ready to defend and serve in any situation. We also work in teams to complete missions and ensure safety for everyone.

Why We Love Our Job:
We love being soldiers because it allows us to be part of something bigger than ourselves. The discipline and strength we've gained are unmatched, and knowing we are protecting our country fills us with pride.

Find Your Path:
In the army, there are many different paths one can take. Some soldiers specialize in technology and communications, while others might focus on medical aid or engineering.

How to Become One of Us?
Becoming a soldier involves both physical and mental preparation. You'll need to pass physical fitness tests and complete rigorous training in a military academy, where you'll learn everything from leadership to combat skills.

A Question for You:
Would you like to wear a uniform and be part of a team that works together to protect your country?

With a heart of valor, strong and grand,
Audie guards our cherished land.
A soldier of might, in unity bound,
Beside Lyudmila, where bravery's found.

 # African Wild Dog

Hey, little guardian! We are Jacquie and Richard, and we are SECURITY GUARDS

Our Key Responsibilities:
As security guards, our main job is to watch over and protect places to make sure everyone is safe. We also help people feel secure by being there to assist them whenever they need.

Why We Love Our Job:
We find joy in being security guards because we play a crucial role in keeping people and properties safe. It's rewarding to know that our presence can make a big difference in ensuring safety and peace.

Find Your Path:
Being a security guard offers a world of variety. Some of us patrol malls, watching over shops and assisting customers, while others safeguard museums, protecting priceless artifacts. We also have the unique role of ensuring the safety of special clients, like celebrities, athletes, or politicians, making sure they're secure wherever they go.

How to Become One of Us?
To become a security guard, start by finishing high school and then receive specific training in security work. This training will teach you how to handle different situations, use security equipment, and provide first aid.

A Question for You:
Imagine having the responsibility of keeping a place safe and sound. Would you like to be the one who watches over and protects it?

Together they patrol, a steadfast pair,
Dedication strong beyond compare.
Richard and Jacquie, in their steady gaze,
Protect and serve in countless ways.

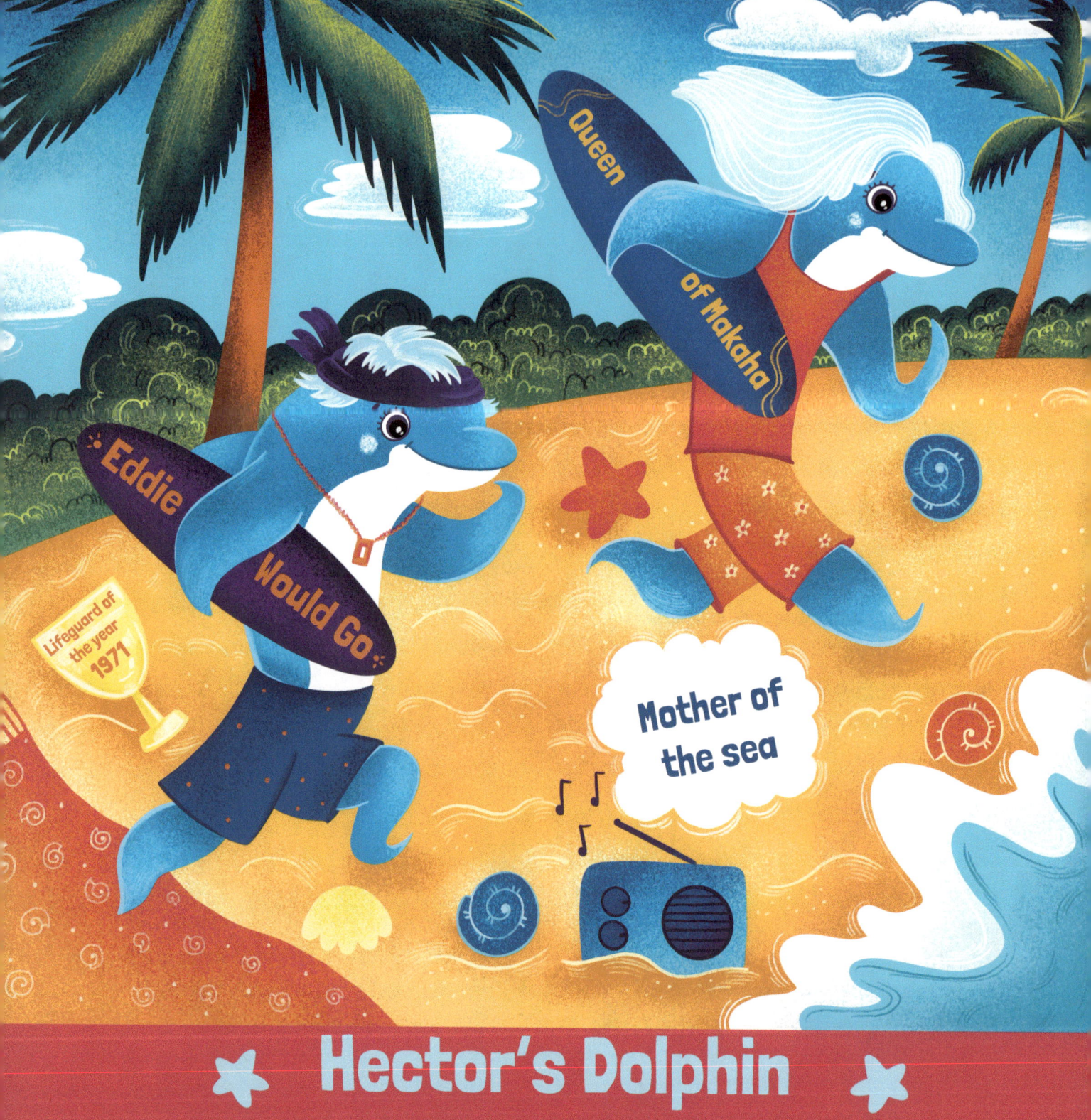

Hello, tiny rescuer! I'm Eddie—and I'm Rell—and we are LIFEGUARDS

Our Key Responsibilities:
Our main task is to watch over swimmers and make sure everyone is safe in and around the water. We are always ready to jump into action to rescue someone if they're in trouble.

Why We Love Our Job:
We adore being lifeguards because it combines our love for swimming with the ability to save lives. There's no better feeling than knowing we've kept someone safe while they enjoy the water.

Find Your Path:
Lifeguarding isn't just about watching pools; we also guard beaches, work on rescue boats, and teach people how to swim safely. Each setting offers unique challenges and rewards.

How to Become One of Us?
To become a lifeguard, you need to be a strong swimmer and pass a lifeguarding course. This course teaches you lifesaving skills like first aid and CPR, preparing you to handle emergencies in the water.

A Question for You:
Can you imagine spending your days by the water, keeping an eye out and ensuring everyone's safety?

Eddie and Rell, by the water's edge,
Watch over swimmers, as they've pledged.
With keen eyes and quick to act,
They ensure no safety's lacked.

Hello, Professor Harvard! What new things will we learn today at the Knowledge Center?

Hello, Grandpa Jobs! Today, we're going to discover how fun learning can be. We'll meet smart people who love to learn and teach.

Can you imagine how exciting it is to discover new things every day? Maybe our young reader will be the one teaching us something new one day!

Let's flip the page and step into a journey of discovery and learning.

Hi, young learner! We are Maria and Jaime, and we are **TEACHERS**

Our Key Responsibilities:
As teachers, we spend our days sharing knowledge and inspiring curiosity in young minds. We create fun lessons that help you learn about the world and guide you in discovering new things.

Why We Love Our Job:
We love being teachers because it's so rewarding to see the lightbulb moments when a student understands something new. Sharing our passion for learning and helping you grow is the best part of our day.

Find Your Path:
Teaching is not just about working in a classroom; teachers can be found in many places, like museums, online, or even outdoors in nature programs. We specialize in different subjects, from math and science to art and music.

How to Become One of Us?
To become a teacher, start by loving to learn. Then, you go to college to study education and the subject you want to teach. After that, you'll practice teaching with the guidance of experienced teachers before you lead your own classroom.

A Question for You:
Would you like to stand in front of a classroom one day, sharing stories and lessons, and watching as your students discover something new?

In their care, young minds grow,
Seeds of thought they carefully sow.
Jaime and Maria, with hearts so grand,
Guide their students to understand.

Hello, little time traveler! You can call us Barbara and Leopold. We are
HISTORIANS

Our Key Responsibilities:
As historians, we explore the past to understand how people lived and what events have shaped our world. We dig through old documents and artifacts to piece together history's puzzles.

Why We Love Our Job:
We adore being historians because it feels like being a time traveler. Discovering stories from the past and sharing them with others is incredibly exciting and fulfilling.

Find Your Path:
Historians don't just work in dusty archives; we can be found teaching at universities, curating in museums, or even making documentaries to bring history to life for everyone.

How to Become One of Us?
To become a historian, start with a love for stories and a curiosity about the past. Studying history in college will help you learn how to research and analyze, and then you can specialize in learning about a particular area of history that fascinates you.

A Question for You:
Could you see yourself as a historian, delving into the past to bring ancient legends and historical events to light?

Together, they illuminate history's lane,
Ensuring the past's not in vain.
Barbara and Leopold, with dedication pure,
Preserve our heritage, to endure.

Greetings, young digger!
I'm Howard and this is my colleague Kathleen, and we are
ARCHEOLOGISTS

Our Key Responsibilities:
As archeologists, we get to explore ancient sites and dig up artifacts that tell us about people who lived long ago. We carefully study these items to learn about past cultures and civilizations.

Why We Love Our Job:
We love being archeologists because every day is an adventure. Uncovering hidden treasures and solving historical mysteries is not just a job; it's a passion that connects us to the ancient world.

Find Your Path:
Archeology is more than just digging in the dirt; we work in labs, write books, and even use technology like drones and satellites to discover new dig sites. Some archeologists even specialize in underwater sites, exploring sunken cities and ships.

How to Become One of Us?
To become an archeologist, you'll need a keen interest in history and a lot of patience. After studying archeology in college, you'll spend time in the field, gaining hands-on experience with excavations and research.

A Question for You:
Can you imagine yourself uncovering lost artifacts and piecing together the stories of ancient civilizations as an archeologist?

Howard and Kathleen, with trowels in hands,
Unearth the stories long buried in sands.
Their digs are a window to ancient days,
Revealing secrets in myriad ways.

.... Pygmy Racoon ....

Hi, future reporter! You can call us Veronica and Joseph. We are JOURNALISTS

Our Key Responsibilities:
As journalists, our job is to discover the truth and share important stories with the world. We interview people, investigate events, and report on news that helps everyone stay informed.

Why We Love Our Job:
We cherish being journalists because it allows us to explore a variety of stories and meet new people. Sharing information that can make a difference in people's lives is truly rewarding.

Find Your Path:
Journalism isn't just about writing articles; we also create documentaries, host podcasts, and report live from events. Journalists can specialize in areas like politics, sports, or science, depending on what fascinates them most.

How to Become One of Us?
To become a journalist, start with a strong curiosity and a love for storytelling. Studying journalism or communications in college teaches you the skills to research, write, and present stories effectively.

A Question for You:
Would you like to be the one asking questions and uncovering stories to share with the world as a journalist?

Veronica and Joseph, watchful and wise,
Capture the world through open eyes.
Together they write to inform and explain,
Ensuring no story remains in vain.

Grey Parrot

My record 71 Translations

Las dos maneras de traducir

Las versiones homéricas

Los traductores de Las mil y una noches

Nikolay G.
Leo T.
Fyodor D.
Ivan T.

The Happy Prince (spanish)

Hola, little communicator! I'm Constance and this is Jorge, and we are TRANSLATORS

Our Key Responsibilities:
As translators, we connect people by helping them to understand each other's words and cultures. We work with written texts, converting documents, books, and articles into another language while keeping their original meaning.

Why We Love Our Job:
We love being translators because it allows us to bridge communication gaps between different cultures. It's deeply fulfilling to translate not just words, but also the emotions and concepts they carry, ensuring people from around the world can connect in a meaningful way.

Find Your Path:
Translation isn't just about working with books; translators are needed in many fields, like business, healthcare, technology, and entertainment. We can also specialize in different types of translation, such as literary, technical, or legal.

How to Become One of Us?
To become a translator, you need a deep love for languages and cultures. Studying languages in college and gaining fluency in at least two languages is essential. Practice and specialized training in translation will help you hone your skills.

A Question for You:
Would you like to connect worlds and help people understand each other by translating languages?

Constance and Jorge, with a careful touch,
Show that translations matter much.
In the labyrinth of language, they hold the key,
Unlocking stories for you and me.

Greetings, young storyteller!
Our names are William, Leo, and Joane, and we are

WRITERS

Our Key Responsibilities:
As writers, our main task is to craft stories and content that entertain, inform, and inspire readers. We brainstorm ideas, develop characters, and weave narratives that capture the imagination.

Why We Love Our Job:
We adore being writers because it allows us to express our creativity and explore endless possibilities through words. Seeing our thoughts come to life on paper and impact readers positively is an incredible feeling.

Find Your Path:
We don't just write novels and poetry; we also work on scripts for movies and plays, articles for magazines, and content for websites. Writers specialize in various genres, from fiction and non-fiction to fantasy and science fiction.

How to Become One of Us?
To become a writer, you should be passionate about storytelling and reading. Practicing your writing regularly and studying literature or creative writing can help improve your skills and understanding of different writing styles.

A Question for You:
Can you imagine creating your own worlds and stories and sharing them with others as a writer one day?

In the realm of words, three scribes do dwell,
Leo, William, Joane; their tales they tell.
With pen in hand, they craft and weave,
Worlds of wonder, they make us believe.

Hi there, tiny genius! We are Albert, Marie, and Isaac, and we are **SCIENTISTS**

Our Key Responsibilities:
As scientists, we explore the mysteries of the universe, conducting experiments and research to discover new knowledge. We study everything from tiny atoms to vast galaxies, always seeking to understand how the world works.

Why We Love Our Job:
We love being scientists because it's like being on a never-ending adventure of discovery. There's always something new to learn, and the thrill of uncovering a secret of the universe is unbeatable.

Find Your Path:
Being a scientist isn't just about working in a lab; we can be found in fields, oceans, and even space. Scientists specialize in various areas, including biology, chemistry, physics, and earth sciences, each contributing to our understanding of the world in different ways.

How to Become One of Us?
To become a scientist, start with a boundless curiosity about the world. Studying science and then specializing in a specific field through college and beyond is crucial. Conducting experiments and publishing our findings helps us share our discoveries with the world.

A Question for You:
Can you picture yourself wearing a lab coat, peering through a microscope, or gazing at the stars, unraveling the mysteries of the world as a scientist?

Albert's theories, deep and vast,
In time and space, a spell he cast.
Marie, with elements, made her mark,
In the glow of radium, a light in the dark.
Isaac, with gravity, explained the fall,
A universal law encompassing all.
Together, their minds a force so precise,
Pioneering paths they did devise.

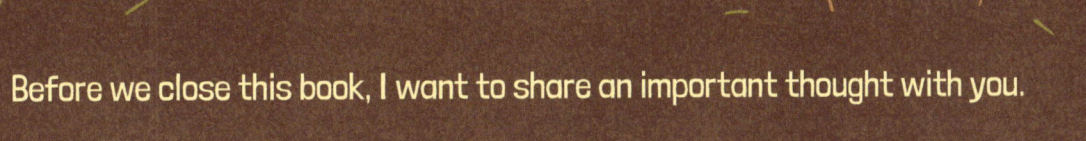

Before we close this book, I want to share an important thought with you.

You may have noticed that there are no people in my magical world of professions—all the workers here are animals. But these are not ordinary animals. They are animals from the Red List, which are endangered species.

Why did I choose them, you may ask?

The world around us is changing rapidly, and every day there are more and more technologies that replace professions. Just as rare animals are gradually disappearing from our lives, some professions are also disappearing, giving way to machines, robots, and new technologies.

This shows us how important it is to take care of not only our natural heritage but also our cultural heritage. Just as we fight to preserve rare animal species, we should also cherish the professions that have shaped our world and our history.

I hope you enjoyed reading this book, and I have one last question for you:

Of all the jobs you learned about today, which one is your favorite?

_____

ANIMAL CONNECTIONS
FOR THE MOST CURIOUS

1. **Doctor** – Snakes are venerated in the legend of Asclepius, the ancient Greek god of healing, symbolizing the enduring connection between medicine and healing practices.

2. **Nurse** – Butterflies fly gracefully from flower to flower, symbolizing the gentle and attentive movement of those who care for patients.

3. **Dentist** – Donkeys are always ready with a smile and have both baby and adult teeth, symbolizing the care required to maintain those smiles throughout different stages of life.

4. **Pharmacist** – Bees gather nectar from various flowers to produce healing honey, symbolizing the careful blending of ingredients to create medicinal remedies.

5. **Psychologist** – Ducks, known for their emotional stability and nurturing presence, symbolize the guiding and transformative role of those who support mental and emotional health.

6. **Veterinarian** – Chimpanzees treat injuries in their community using ant gel, symbolizing the instinctive care and healing practices found in nature.

7. **Zookeeper** – Pandas, a recognized symbol of wildlife conservation, embody the spirit of those dedicated to the care and preservation of animals.

8. **Police Officer** – Snapping shrimps use one of their claws as a pistol to stun prey or defend themselves, symbolizing the role of those tasked with protection and maintaining order.

9. **Firefighter** – Elephants, which use their trunks to spray water in situations such as fire or to cool themselves, embody a natural form of firefighting.

10. **Soldier** – Rhinoceroses, known for their strength and powerful presence, symbolize those who stand strong and powerful in their roles.

11. **Security Guard** – Wild dogs, known for their protective instincts within the pack, embody a natural form of guarding and safety.

12. **Lifeguard** – Dolphins are known to save people's lives in the ocean, symbolizing the vigilant and rescue-oriented nature of those who watch over swimmers.

13. **Teacher** – Owls are a symbol of wisdom and intelligence, embodying the qualities essential for those who educate and guide others.

14. **Historian** – Sharks, one of the longest-lived animals on Earth, have witnessed centuries of history, embodying the enduring nature of those who study and preserve our past.

15. **Archeologist** – Prairie dogs, known for their diligent digging, symbolize the persistent and exploratory nature of those who unearth history.

16. **Journalist** – Raccoons explore and dig through their environments, symbolizing the inquisitive and investigative nature of those who delve into stories and uncover information.

17. **Translator** – Parrots can mimic various sounds and voices, symbolizing the ability to bridge communication between different languages, much like those who translate words and meanings across cultures.

18. **Writer** – Geese, whose feathers were historically used as quills, symbolize the traditional tools that brought words to life on paper.

19. **Scientist** – Bonobos, which are closely related to humans and represent a key figure in studies of evolution, symbolize the pursuit of scientific knowledge and understanding of our own origins.

www.ingramcontent.com/pod-product-compliance
Lightning Source LLC
LaVergne TN
LVHW062123171224

799308LV00015B/302